In Search of Sanity

Ruby Hoffman

BookLeaf Publishing

India | USA | UK

Presentation by *BookLeaf Publishing*

Web: www.bookleafpub.com

E-mail: info@bookleafpub.com

ISBN: 9789363314177

First edition 2024

I would like to dedicate this book to my 9th grade English teacher Katherine Moffat, since deceased. During each class, she encouraged us to see beyond the mundane and to build upon the many inferences we could draw from the literature we delved into and the lives we lived. I am grateful for her belief in us as students and the legacy she created.

ACKNOWLEDGEMENT

Thank you to my family and friends for supporting me in my growth as a person to this point and for pushing me to reach beyond my limitations to fill new spaces while we learn from each other.

PREFACE

This collection of poetry is divided into six segments--the Odes, the Sonnets, the Haiku, the Glosas, the Sestinas and the Prose. Each work is interconnected by the core exploration of the human conscience.

With each new day, we face individualized quests. Who am I in light of my values? What do my principles motivate me to do for my community? When did I become molded to the figure I inhabit today? Where can I traverse from here? Why can discontentment seep into the joyful soul? How will I find fulfillment in a life that has grown overcast with cloud?

When I was recently traveling in Japan, a friend shared an interesting illustration drawn around a dandelion. She shared that, in the case of such a delicate sprout, 'the harder the winds blow, the more growth you will see' as new flowers emerge from planted, drifting seeds. On the journey through life's difficulties and obstacles we can feel like helpless dandelions on a windy day; yet, it is from these experiences of trial that we can witness growth through endurance and emerge "complete and sound in all respects, not lacking in anything" (James 1:2-4; NWT). Let us reflect as we persevere together.

Ode to a Cloud

Oh voluminous, towering wonder--
a blanket on the sky's bare surface are you!

To be encircled by the fondling embrace
of your soft skin;
To have certain safety in the lofty haven
of your abode.

Oh cloud, how you fly high:
so majestically as you bend and spread
upon the wind's touch.

Yet you do not give out your weight for
my life to be taken, crushed and cracked
forever;
You float, instead, to enlighten my mind
with each new form you take.

Ode to Sunrise

A depth of darkness
uncharted, unassuming, impenetrable.
until--
A faint light emerges
a hazy hue behind the clinging veil of night
until--
the veil rises
and
a mighty glow begins to peel across the horizon
like victory.
The face of the Sun is
seen.
A scene so unlike that which held us captive
moments before
in the incorrigible ferocity of the darkest hour.
Oh, sunrise!
You gentle giant of the day...
Your beloved light dances upon the surface of
the open skies
illuminating surrounding truth,
broadening perspective,
revealing:
the limitations of the night are not eternal;
the forward motion of each new day bestows
promise;

and
as we question obscurities in the night we train
our eyes to perceive
an unexpected, unspoken, intangible beauty in
the clarity we find
at daybreak.

Ode to Sunset

Oh the entrancing,
dynamic power
of your many forms!
the careful handiwork of an artist and his brush
are you.
Blinding, piercing light you shed on the eyes of
your beholders.
Beholden to the energy of your fading warmth,
the clouds absorb your light and
as cotton candy plumes they remain.
After your illumination has fallen beneath the
landscape of day,
beckoning "tomorrow and tomorrow and
tomorrow,"
the nightingale breaks into song.

Ode to Music

The poetry of sound,
the oracle of intuition;
To be seen in your songs,
to be met by your melodies,
rich rhythms,
and rhymes.
Oh, the solace of your perceptivity!
A connecting force for the human course, are
you--
inviting lovers,
friends,
and foes
into the warm abode of fresh harmony.
You bestow contentment in the notion that all is
not lost,
the future is vast,
inspiration abounds
as your effusions fill the souls of weary travelers
in life's procession.
Together, we learn to find music in the motions
of living.
We whistle while we work to
bide long hours
long after mothers' lullabies have faded into
distant memories of peace since past.

We young can be wise
We old can be youthful
We of all walks of life come together in the
singular pursuit
of the companionship
of this art
of yours.

Ode to Espresso

Oh, the aroma you exude
on a slothful morning of
a lingering tomorrow--
You bolster confidence,
imbuing the senses with refreshment and energy
like a new day.
You free the senses to soar in a cloud land of
daydreams and
optimism.
The careful crafting of your body into differing
delectables
fills the cup of a weary soul
with innovation, passion, spontaneity, childlike
wonder;
each sip turning jadedness to glimmering jade
reversing taciturnity for a tickle in the soul
laughter bellowing forth,
jazzing!
Each moment is fresh and whole--

Sonnet I

Deformity of mind, body and soul-
innate plights of the carefree wanderer.
All wearied by the weight of man's control,
her innovations test each ponderer.

Parading into unknown parts of yore
--a journey, an adventure for the soul--
to find the truth of all which lies in store,
for long life is as yet our very goal.

Precipitation comes from clouds above
and carries life to flowers here below;
so, trav'ling tinker is consumed with love
from whence the buds of passion are to grow.

A life of one whose end arrived too soon
yet casts a light like night receives from moon.
<3

Sonnet II

A raindrop falls on her uncovered head--
a storm to overtake the afternoon;
Instead of rolling into her soft bed,
she ponders over obstacles unhewn.

A writing table where she oft' has sat
and broken chair to hold her aching bones,
are all the semblance of today's format...
Embracing solace in the storm's soft tones

Predictability is hard to find
in the unceasing storm of daily life.
Her joy and desolation intertwined,
she looks within to heal pervading strife

An afternoon of spontaneous bliss
to understand just what she does now miss.

Sonnet III

A second time is never quite the same
Since tainted by her failures in past lots.
However she may redirect her claim,
morbidity's unyielding as it plots.

Each newfound love is fresh like morning dew--
bestowing hope, the winged feathered thing.
Enlightening the mind to prospects new,
variety invites her heart to sing.

Adventure in a world of dreams ahead
combats cacophonies of fearful "no"s,
removing every trace of needless dread
as life becomes again a flow'r that grows.

A blossom in a field of many weeds,
she lives to brightens lives by meeting needs.

Sonnet IV

Her new persona bears a ling'ring scar;
in tests of tribulation was it born.
Each stride with which she steps sets a new
par…
Resiliency enables her to warn.

Impoverished by carelessness, mistrust,
she found nowhere to turn when grapes did sour.
Her lonesome solitude collected dust
as if she failed to see her gleaming power!

The sun still shines for day to bring us light,
and vitamins do vitalize the veins;
therefore to spread inner joy instills might
in those still battling prevailing pains.

We share a space called life, in broken molds,
together facing strife and reaching goals.

Sonnet V

To hear the voice of one you cannot see,
in whispers of the mind that say: "go on,"
in life's work triggering a memory,
and filling saddened hearts with hopeful song.

Her life moves onward in the grasp of grief;
new joys peel through the curtain of remorse.
Determination bolsters firm belief
that peace is near if she does stay course.

For she is not alone—though she held doubt—
surrounded by support that does abound.
Emerge, beloved, from this unseemly bought,
and bask in present joy, which you have found!

Just as the moon shines on the darkest night,
companionship dispels the murk of fright.

An Early Blossom's Haiku

13

Coldest wintry night--
the blooming sakura tree,
promises of spring.

Haiku in the Fields

Strawberry patches
ripe and ready for picking,
warmest summer breeze.

Life's Garden Haiku

15

Fresh vegetables
in a garden of living;
satisfying meals.

Haiku of the Wind

Windy seaside air,
waves tempestuous and free
against the shore's plain.

Moon Beam's Haiku

Moon beams brighten eyes
their rays remind me of us
in the night's abyss.

Glosa I: Hoping

"Hope" is the thing with feathers -
That perches in the soul -
And sings the tune without the words -
And never stops - at all -
- Emily Dickinson, "'Hope' is the thing with
feathers"

While I wait in shock, I abhor absence
—feeling alone is like abandonment—
in the piercing darkness of self loathing,
as despair rests on untamed jealousy…
Yet! I have that which perches on the soul,
ever singing a tune that strengthens bones,
ever fortifying the weak—onward.
Within me it calls that others, too, need
to be shielded from throwing of stones,
to wait together between sighs and groans.

Life is moving so quickly as we wait
—the days bleed into weeks and months to
years—
long days forget the Hope that sings within,
as the aching emptiness carves a hole
whereon the winged thing would once have
perched.

Brilliantly beautiful memories, say:
"Adventures lie ahead, still yet unknown!"
Our winged thing rejoins the weary soul,
-it never stopped at all- and guides the way.
"Keep separate from the broken, battered fray."

Emerge from the mind's cavernous closure,
from Calypso's Cave on homebound journey,
to hear again the song -the lovely lark-
as it perches gently on throbbing heart.
Travels are aimless until we have Hope,
until we gaze forward to land each step.
No words does she sing -mysteri'us wing'd
thing-
as she fills the soul with incandescent
Peace, like new day's sunrise--welcomed and
wept.
Deep breaths in calm, revitalizing reps.

Taking a seat in the present moment,
taste the heartening sensations
of the now -the flavorful fleetingness-
Relish the rays of sun seeping into
your blemished skin -infusing light and life-
Allow the feathered thing to rest.
While waiting for relief of rejoinder,
listening to the breeze as it blows through
yesteryear's trees -standing beyond time's test-
Hope hires endurance in each dying breast.

Glosa II: Arising

"Just like moons and like suns,
With the certainty of tides,
Just like hopes springing high,
Still I'll rise."
-Maya Angelou, "Still I Rise"

In the escapade of life, borne along
by pieces of recognition -aha!-
to feel as though we have understanding,
and to float along the clouds of notions
that we are something great, something known,
we fall from the heights we've reached in our
pride
to level earth… then rise. We walk onward.
Beyond the bouts and barriers of dread,
rise to see the light of moons with each stride
—companionship with the stoic night's bride.

Stillness in the lonesome moments of thought
as we rise, looking for suns in the gloom
of uncertainty. -What do I know, now?-
Now. A space in time marked by the knowledge
of expectations dashed and moves forward.
Forward. Learning from the confidences cracked
neath crushing weight of Reality's hand.

Hand. I'm dealt a hand of cards, a game;
yet, life's not a game, it is a gift—backed
by loving and being beloved, as fact.

Be alive and believe in betterment,
in the certainty of the tides to soon
peel over the shore in constant motion;
then see a new day wherein others rise
-too- together singing a song of hope
through the breeze that rolls along the shoreline
with coming tides of restful resemblance.
Common humanity is found through trial,
each one discerning shortfalls to refine—
to rise from failings, prone supine.

Indeed we fall again and over, on
unfamiliar rocks of untraversed paths—
universal cyclicality. Rise!
Others have, in eternity's landscape,
floundered in and followed life's rugged
course—
rising like high-springing hopes to new strength.
Fortified by overturned misgivings,
revitalizing views to camaraderie,
we learn to aid each other at great lengths
to rise from our sorrows as soothed by nepenthe.

Decision's Sestina

Impelled by lively notions,
novelty of being, effervescence—
I wonder if a divergent roadway
leaves room for retracing in some future
or marks this life with stains of decision,
indefinite binding of soul to foul work.

Cruel fate to detest one's work!
Anticipating promised false notions,
like validation can bless decision…
-doubt not the might of pure effervescence! -
Attempts to obscure a promising future
are obstacles on the untraced roadway.

It is this chosen roadway,
life's pathway making broken pieces work.
Human connection, creating futures—
Together, trampling crushing notions
of "not enough…" to be effervescent!
Camaraderie rebuffs indecision.

Emotional decisions,
each stumbling blocks on the open roadway
— racing to be praised for effervescence,
careening into a new load of work—

undesired, tiresome, confounding notions.
Failures train our minds for better futures.

Dancing promise of future,
inspiring confidence in Decision,
moves the body to spin new notions
-o'er the rainbow lie yellow-brick roadways-
Places unexplored are like fresh artwork
in a studio of effervecence.

Compelled to effervescence,
we travel toward untested futures—
learning humanity's aid is real work,
life's community builder is Decision.
Assisting others paves unmet roadways;
rising choices still challenge self-notion.

Misunderstood, miscellaneous notions
peel across the mind along the roadway.
Mortal clouds cast defensive decisions.

Sestina by the Sea

I wade, knee-deep, through sea,
along an envied shore. My feet are bare.
Thinking of what made me full when I ate...
how later when I journal I will write
of how I'm full and what I shouldn't buy.
Water rushes over my feet in waves.

Envisioning kindly waves,
with sincerest smiling, when I see
your freed face glowing, as in days gone by.
What does it matter what burdens I bear?
Now that you're with me the world's become
right.
I am whole, notwithstanding what I ate.

Remembering when I arrived at eight,
-yearning for connection under Grief's waves-
We imagined adventures, setting rights...
-golden mem'ries my nostalgia can see-
as I reconstruct remembrance, left bare.
Endless laughs and dreaming before good-bye.

I didn't want to say the last goodbye.
It crushed my chest, like what I never ate.
Suffocating hunger, heart nearly bare,

nearly consoled by fellow grievers' waves…
Those too, carried farewell—Past off to sea.
A world wherein wrong triumphs over right.

Numb in the brokenness, write,
in open reminiscence by the by,
of your courageous journeys across seas.
The enjoyment of living as you ate,
filling new friends with good tidings in waves,
never leaving without cov'ring what's bare.

Drawn back to the beach, with "Bear,"
I notice a dog at play to my right.
To be alive in worlds of joys and waves,
a gift no amount of money can buy…
Forever is ahead, like lasting eight,
unending Peace, as constant as the Sea.

Endless rejoinder in Life we will see,
supping together, fretting not what we ate.
Sorrowing's past as beloved ones stand by.

Violet's Storm

The exterior window is covered with sheets of
water
from the incumbent rainstorm. A suitable
summer's day.
Inside, Violet takes shelter from the shadows of
swirling skies
while she composes daydreams to the tempo of
the dithering droplets—
Grave… adagio… allegro! … adagio… Vivace!
Then, thunderous percussion as bolts of
lightning pierce the sky!
Never needing the rains to cease as the music of
her soul swells
in a Storm of new thought—blooming.
Thoughts trickle toward seasons ahead.
When summer ends and fall lends beauty to
deterioration by winter.
Why will time not freeze in the expanse of this
enjoyment, in the foyer of freeness, in the
guesthouse of growth—
to stay contented in the shelter of the Now?
Complaining "what-if"s resolve nothing as the
clouds release their readying rains, for
tomorrow's blossoms.

Violet, too, is new, storm-filled, beautiful—a
breathtaking, pulchritudinous dame in a world
full of summers' days.
As the storm stills
-adagio… grave-
she steps outside, umbrella-less,
to splash soundingly along that familiar road
whereby new purple-petaled shoots have sprung
up,
to drink for their sun-filled future;
and she dances with the promising Purples in the
lingering winds of
this sublimest storm--
fresh with the purplish shoots of freedom in her
soul, in the vivacity of the Violet to be.

Among the Peonies, Forever

Gazing across a panoply of peonies, a lone
woman ponders her past,
painting newness.
A fraction of her mind, a memory's fringes, a
tangible proof of the present—her gift.
Her brush strokes sail smoothly and fall to
flourishes as the sun glistens across her field, her
muse.
Pensive among the peonies, she hones her craft.
Home:
a figment of her imagination, a state of inmost
contentment, a sense of place—wherever.
She is lost… Lost in thought. Lost in the motion
of the bending plumes of peonies along the
horizon.
Her canvas is darkening as the sun fades in pinks
and oranges to hazy grey blues to end the day.
Settling into the discomfort of waning visibility,
she sets down the day's last strokes, leaving
hints of what's inhabited her mind's eye.
In a space continuum of Time, once the night
has fallen, she lingers to feel the empty breeze
and listen to the whispers of the peonies as their
agile backs fold under its breaths. They will
linger a time, and soon too will fade in pinks and

oranges to the grey browns of the underlying
soil, for next year's Newness.
How, then, does she find enjoyment in the now,
knowing?
She meanders in the meadows of memory, in the
haziness of holding on, in the waiting on the
surety of the fresh season which will soon come
and grace the greensward with what's Missing.
Her gaze is fixed now on the stars
and she breathes in and out in peace, as the
winds blow the last air of her mind's journey off
to a distant place where
today's work is done.
Resting reflectively for the unforeseen Next, she
hums a soft tune for the peonies
a youthful lullaby that grows in the pastures of
her mind, in her pink and orange paints, in her
grey, pencil-stained hands, in her windswept,
brown hair, in the luminaries of the night.
A painting of a lived-in moment
lives on like a lone woman
among the peonies, forever.

www.ingramcontent.com/pod-product-compliance
Lightning Source LLC
LaVergne TN
LVHW010839200726
843508LV00012B/2660